AF560497

Rhythm of the Ruins

Rhythm of the Ruins

Poems by

Mukul Kumar

THE BROWSER
www.thebrowser.org
Publishers & Booksellers

Rhythm of the Ruins
by
Mukul Kumar

First Published in India in 2022
by J.G.S. Enterprises Pvt. Ltd.
Imprint: The Browser

Publisher's Address:
SCO 14-15, FF, Sector 8-C, Chandigarh 160 009
Email: service@thebrowser.org

Edition: I
ISBN: 978-93-92210-04-4

Printed in India

www.thebrowser.org
Publishers & Booksellers

Dedicated to my Father (1934-2021)

A Tribute
(I miss you terribly, Papa)

Papa

He so pours affection from
His unlimited bowl,
A canopy ever expanding
That shades my earth whole.

My sky stretches, serene
Within the fortress of his care,
Deluge or draught draws from
My shelter a joyous smug stare.

Of this nectar, an ounce less,
I would disdain, an ounce more,
I would dismiss; perfection
Allows neither less nor more.

What when you are no more,
The grief that mind has never known,
A crisis existential, when the being
Is taken over by the Unknown.

Contents

Foreword

Mukul Kumar's poetry covers a wide range of themes and emotions: from the appreciation of the luminous divine mystery embedded in every scene in nature to the scandalous poverty perceived in a Bombay slum. The poems have a rare cadence and sonority that comes from a genuine feeling for words and reveal a powerful visual imagination that captures sights in their vivid detail and extracts their hidden poetry. Love, death, nature, reconciliation: there is hardly any aspect of existence or any state of the human mind left untouched by the poet's omniscient pen.

—K. Satchidanandan (Internationally acclaimed poet and critic)

Acknowledgements

First and foremost, a debt of gratitude to my father who played a seminal role in the formation and maturation of my literary sensibility.

My mother, wife, and lovely aughter, have always been, visibly or invisibly, by my side encouraging me on through my literary journey.

I extend sincere thanks to my dear friend Payel Roy Chowdhury who has been a great support with her valuable suggestions regarding the various aspects of my work.

Pawan and Khushi Ram have extended crucial support in the venture. I am grateful to my Service for all the possible support to realise my creativity.

Pankaj P. Singh and the team of The Browser, of course, who made this work reach the readers.

And last but not the least, I owe special gratitude to K. Satchidanandan and Prof. Sanjukta Dasgupta for blessing my book with blurbs!

Mukul Kumar

A Testimony to Divinity

The spring winds stir in the boughs
Setting them into quiet quiver,
Caress my ears with
A sweet, sonorous whisper,
And rustle over me, and I rejoice this
Sheath of a nameless pleasure.
Birds flit in the hedges and bushes to
Set them off into the tremor of thrill, and
Hop and peck about in a wide wonder,
Their chirps and chirrups echoing the silences.
Bees buzz around, and butterflies hover
With a frenetic freedom, unlocking a
Curious wanderlust in me.
My wondered being, nimble and wide,
Thirsting for more, travels to the
Sky that is radiant, celestial with the
Liquid gold, the iridescent clouds,
Misshapen and mesmerising,
Wandering, galore and gay, and
The starlings and the birds unknown
Fly wide-winged on their way.
The noon wanes, and into the gold
Infuses some dark silver, and around
The ball of fire, orange, lavender,
Turquoise and what not turns the
Iridescent grey, and the birds
In droves get set in spray.

Time turns winged, and the mood gets
Steeped in an ecstatic melancholy,
And I am moved, motionless,
Awakened into a sublime slumber,
When the senses unite to serve the spirit, and
The divine faith demands no demonstration.

Dreaming Anarchy

The debris of a castle heaped in
A stately house now weighs heavy;
It is completely crumbled under the
Crushing weight of the orders that have
Closed in, the grand soulless structures
Ruled by the faceless Czars.

The motions of living are slowing,
The felicity for a smile that masks a
Sigh is falling fragile, the senses
Now rendered too senile to disallow
The soul its long due rise, its glimmer,
The dusk that is sister to dawn, and the
Face and feel in a messy mingle.

I am caught up in the eddying currents
That are set sweeping within, the look
And feel the prelude to a cataclysm;
Heaven shows itself through the skies
That split with thunder and lightning.
Universe was created with a bang;
I am eagerly waiting for the anarchy
That can rebuild my castle.

The Manticore

An infant in the throes of
Helpless tears is perched atop
The bosom of the mother, his
Frantic nudges to wake her up
Unanswered, his hungry cries
Amplifying the macabre silence;
The life is too young to learn of death;
Sleep and death are synonyms.
On platter is blood, not milk;
Death has just finished its dance,
An ominous hiatus may be,
The corpses littered on the
Sheet of blood, torn or smeared,
The bosom of the bombed earth
Bleeding with a terrible tremor.
A toddler's tears are tireless,
The scream sends the silence into
A cacophonous crescendo.

The tremor mutates into quake, as
A manticore* prowls around, the earth
Groaning under its lurid limbs; its eyes
Snigger a terrible victory, the looks
Shining thirsty for the blood still on
The platter, and the tail wagging in a
Gory glee to suck out the life that
Is left gasping.

The arrival upon the child, silenced
With shock, the tears trapped in
His incarcerated sighs.
Horror trips the trajectory of
The imagination.

*A manticore is a Persian legendary creature that has the head of a human, the body of a lion and the tail of venomous spines or of a scorpion.

Mirror Pairs Psyche with Narcissus

A crisis threatens my love for the
Meditation on my mirror reflection—
The smug smile flitting on the face, the
Acknowledgment of a house well-kept,
Replenished the wind for the sail
When the world betrayed.

The gaze no more returns from the
Body; time is sipping the dew off
The blossom, and the light tends to
Travel deeper, suddenly really deep
Now; a strange reflection stares at me
From the mirror, challenging my
Cognition; a curious consternation
Unsettles me, the rise of the surreal.

A soothing courage lights up
My eyes to brave the stare of the
Reflection—the bliss from the
Loving embrace of the charming
Psyche, her beatific smile the loveliest
Butterfly that imagination could
Conjure. The cognition returns.
It's Psyche pairing with Narcissus;
Narcissus embalms the bruises he
Inflicted on Psyche, and she
Repentantly kisses the scars of

I Spill the Missing Breast Milk

As I pass by a shanty in the Dharavi slum,
Where I am to buy myself a
Leather jacket, an unconscious sight
Strikes me hard, plucking me from the
Enthusiasm—the excitement of an addition to
My variegated wardrobe;
A woman suckling her new-born,
Unmindful of the exposure, her
Femininity robbed of coyness by
The classic arms of poverty; the
Child frantically sucked the breast
That looked distastefully shrivelled, for
The milk that was not there.

The colour of the milk that I spilt
The same morning—the glass toppled
By an unmindful hand engaged in an
Entertaining mobile—changes to blood
Red in the mind that is a Crab Nebula
Now; it is her blood that couldn't be
Mutated into milk for her breast;
The hallucination churns me, filling in
The horrific pity on my
Belief in socialism and
Knowledge of welfare economics.

The Sublime Syzygy

The Sun and the Moon adorn the
Sky at once, kissing-close, as the
Sunset and the moonrise unite at
This delicate hour, the gentlest hues of
Birth and Death merging, a mushy
Magnificence, the golden Moon,
The beloved, blushing gold at the
Sudden sight of her lover that holds
His last breath for her glance.

Rises in the mind Michelangelo's
God forcing the Sun and the Moon
Apart at their birth, on the
Sistine Chapel ceiling—
A leaf from the Book of Genesis.
How blissful is this revelatory spectacle
Of the rebellious union, and
God's submission to the
Magic of Nature, and power of Love!

Wanderlust

The summit sublimates into the mist
That drifts into the clouds around;
Its rise, gay and spirited, speaks of the
Thirst for the sky, the unknown, freed
From the dreary fixity of the abode;
Knowledge is the enemy to discovery,
And nothing can be everything.
The sight echoes in my heart, with
All its magic and merriment, and in all
Its spirits and shades.

The unspotted sky swoons over the sea,
Arching to kiss it with an unafraid
Passion; the sublime blue horizon, the
Two blues echoing each other,
Beckons me with its surreal charm;
The loveliest journey is to an illusory
Destination, when an untiring adventure
Colours the quest for discovery, fatigue
And fervour fuse into the bliss of
Freedom, and travels and arrives
Every rowing.

The sky is a beautiful bowl resting
Delicately upon the brilliant golden
Saucer of an unending desert; the
Harrowing hollowness is enticing; the

Rapidly shifting dunes under the
Fearsome roaring winds inspire the
Terrible charm of mutability;
The eerie enchantment calls me aloud,
Excitement turning and tossing within
With a wild gayness; God and Ghost
Are twins, and fear is the pet of the
Unadulterated freedom. One of the
Chimeras has to be oasis; faith is the
Feather for flight.

The forest is enveloped in darkness,
The moonlight seducing it into
Alluring colours, curves and contours;
The femme fatale foments in me a
Fatal attraction; fright is the spice of
Adventure, danger the darling of
Discovery and terror the trinket of
Beauty; on offer is nature
At its surreal best, with the whispers
Of ghostly silences, strange
Sounds of the sleeping forest, and the
Spooky Smells of prowling beasts, that
Is sure to be the cure of the malignant
Malady of Monotony.

Craving for Catharsis

Overcast bosom,
But smoky eyes;
Cloud does seek the ordained cooling
To rain, that constant heat
Renders infeasible.
Ah, I wish a hiatus in the heat,
Not an escape!
Catharsis is the eternal language
Of my bliss; with time I have learnt
How to embrace the truth.

Waiting for the Storm

The summer was beginning to
Feel well arrived, the Sun sizzling to
The sweaty extent, nature
Blanching the eyes, a slumberous
Stillness setting in and the sounds
In distance amplifying the silence.

Lying comatose post a carefree,
Sumptuous lunch, I sense my bleary
Mind blazing with a surreal vision;
Life, living, dreams, desires—the
Messy mix looms large, the shades of
Fulfillment and failures in riots;
A nebula that feels
Bizarre beyond definition.

The sudden rustle of the mild storm
Rouses me into excitement, the
Senses stirred, and body enlivened;
The sight of the darkening ether,
Blowing winds, swinging boughs, and
Clouds gathering gaily fill the mind with
Exhilaration and also a poignant
Craving for the storm that could sparkle
My soul that is long steeped in slumber.

Everything Is Actually Nothing

My every breath is perfect,
Its vigour and volume impeccable;
Life is an intoxication, impregnable,
When the ride can only be joyous.

I am gasping for breath that
Refuses to be kind to its host;
The shreds of my vanity are
The splinters of a mirror that just
Beamed blissfully Euphrosyne, that
Lie embedded into my lacerations.

From the bliss to the inferno
There is only a flash!

Venus de Milo Comes Alive in Full

She is caught up in the sudden
Burst of the rains, the sky shooting
Torrents, as if the cloudsa are in conspiracy.
Soaked to the skin, her contours rise
In their sensuous splendour, her
Graceful bearing in an erotic radiance.
Rain is such a prodigious sculptor!
As wetness fashions her statuesque,
And sets her chiselled face into
A quivering blush, the teeming pearls
Adorning her gleaming neck that is
The picture of a beautied slenderness,
My nerves are set afire, and
Imagination turns the playground of
Sinful fantasies, the water feeding
The desperate flames.
But the trail of such a wild
Sparkle is a mere pulsating stillness, as
Mars and Apollo get engaged into
A passionate duel within.

We Define Love

Each time we meet, you rob
A little of myself; but then losing is
Not loss always; the same you
Fills in to render me bigger, brighter;
The Sun-shot cloud, iridescent, an
Enchanting stroke of spectral hues;
Suffusion is inherently expansive.
The confluence of the two is
Neither of the two—a new
Creature into being.
'Love is Divine' is not an imaginary
Flight of a philosophical mind,
It is an experiential dwelling of
A material heart!

I Breathe Melancholy

I am everything I wished not to be!
Half a thing is worse than nothing.
Fulfillment is my passion, and
Self-love craving.
As I seek the world,
The world eludes my possession.
Character is destiny; self-loathing
Burgeons within to inundate the
World within. I am a picture of
A splintered mirror;
Oh, how painful it is to be
Condemned to incomplete reflections!
I move about within the Tartarus,
Clueless, enveloped in the clouds of
Unwept pain.
But even the wildest of wanderings
Has a destination; I get cast by
A placid silvery lake, sensing
A bizarre emergence.
The melancholic waters tosses
A complete reflection.
Narcissus takes a pleasurable
Turn within!

The Rhythm of the Ruins

A nebulous mass is gnawing
At my heart with an unrelenting
Unfeelingness; the cloud refuses to
Rain, the catharsis remains elusive;
Emotions seek thoughts, and
Thoughts words, hopelessly.
It's a lull after the storm, a
Cacophonous silence, deafening,
A void filling in me, harrowing;
It will endure, no matter time is
The healer; life loves defying
The proverb as it is Life.
I am fashioning myself to move
About well in the 'Chaos', as anarchy
Assumes a new order—
The rhythm of the ruins.
But still I wish the birth of
'Gaia' and 'Eros' to bless me with
A new order.

The Effortless Adventure

A long, really long, tunnel of
Darkness, interspersed with
The short tunnels of light, never
Long enough for blindness to
The darkness, and far and few,
Always; the portrait of life that
My experiences have endorsed.

Now, while I traverse through the
Pathway of life, I can envision
The last tunnel, lighted or dark,
With the dead end.

The beyond is an uncertain
Nothingness; when reality sets,
Imagination rises. If adventure is the
Spice of life, uncertainty is the Spice
Of adventure.
Death is such an effortless
Adventure!

The Transfiguration

Lying in my bed, I watch playing on
The window screen of my room,
Nature in its myriad hues,
Light and darkness dancing to
The diurnal rotation of the earth,
The hubbub of living, and the
Lub-dub of heart taking their turns
Along the cycle of day and night,
The silence and the sounds
Echoing each other as the sight
Seeps from the eyes into the soul,
And metamorphoses into vision.

Nature would still be playing
On this window box even when
The pair of eyes on the bed ceases
To exist; Nature would still be
Playing if all the pairs of eyes in
The Universe would cease to exist.

It's a journey from the Titan to the
Twerp; the twerp that turns aware
That it's always on the cliff;
Constant threat is fear fearsome
No more;
In the glow of epiphany the twerp
Is transfigured into Titan, David

Juxtaposed against Goliath.
Living an aware life is the finest
Act of chivalry.

The Philosophy of Love

The spectre of separation haunts her
Desire for union, the mind planted as
The guard of the heart that is set for
A leap; the dried tears have smeared
Her vision for the heart.

Let her know, the pain-smitten duo will
Unite on the bed of melancholy, where
The resonance of warmth thaws
The frozen sadness into tears;
The irrigation of the souls for the
Sowing of love.

Let her witness, the finest hue of love
Rises on the horizon where desire
Bows to kiss the wounds, passion
Raining upon pain to
Transfigure it into ecstasy.

Let her realise, transfiguration is a
Phenomenon transient, flash is
Fleeting, ecstasy is expressed in
Tears, and salvific love is cathartic,
That graces not the seekers of
Pleasure, but the practitioners of pain.

Unison

An automatic engagement of bodies,
Flat to frenzy in a flash, the fetishes
Discovering their own magical powers,
Nerves live wires, and
Blood a hot raging stream;
Transfiguration into the treasurehouse
Of surreal sensations, the senses
Charmed into the serpentine voyage
That is buoyed by an agonising
Ardency, and perishes into roaring
Raptures, the fizz engulfing the shore.
It is the solitary earthly theatre of
Transcendence!

The Luminous Night

As I take a slumberous turn,
The smeary eyes sense the
Dawn stealing into my room,
The silver-infused darkness,
An awakened silence,
A stirred stupefaction that rues
The Sun-blotted Moon, and seeks
The total eclipse again, a voyage
Into parallel realities, the realm
Of beauty; night burns to flame the
Darkness that lights up dream;
Let the night linger to gift me the
Sleep under this gleam.

The New Year Eve (December 2021)

A delicate stance on the fence
Between the past and the future,
The proverbial ideal of living in
The present in dissolution;
A celebratory departure from the
Living philosophy.
The hapless 31st December groans
Under a sobbing past and
A sober future, shorn of the
Sparkle of the glorious promises;
Hope otherwise also looks Mona Lisa,
A smile smothered with suspicion.
I have stretched my arms wide open
To welcome the new year, meditating
Upon equanimity, not ecstasy;
The glow of destiny upon man is
Not the certain sunrise, but the
Uncertain spectrum.

The Redemption of Sisyphus

The silence speaks,
The stillness moves;
The severance from reality is
The swing into fantasy where
Solitude finds the company of
The Bluebirds, a redeeming escape
From the Sisyphus within; the chirrups
Find an instant echo with my soul, as
I am embowered in a togetherness,
Sweet and serene, when the mind
Unburdens the image of the
Porcupines huddled together to
Escape the fate of annihilation.
I manage to live on the hope of
This life from the death of reality.

The Discovery of Love

The Pandemic destroys the meeting of
Lovers; the pang of separation
Brings the fate of an unrealised love;
Did the unison of senses not bless us
With the climactic hue of love? The
Eyes darkened with a burning desire,
That spoke the craving for an instant
Possession, the feverish breaths that
Told the racing hearts, the red passions
That coursed in us, the embers
Swinging into embrace to create a
Captivating conflagration where played
The union of the Serpents of Desire, the
Touch, taste and aroma of our beings
Feeding the fire to a frenzy, and
Finally, the white ecstasy that glowed
Upon the bodies, the theatres of a
Stormy lull, as the mind and heart
Engaged in a rare moment of
Symphonic concord, and the silence
That sang the song of a satiated love,
A melody divine.

Now we are robbed of all except the
Desperate eyes and ears to see and
Hear each other in a world, virtual,
That is shorn of the vitality to stage a

Fulfilled love. Ah today, tomorrow, and
The many morrows to come, all seem
Painted alike! But the journey belies
The knowledge and the experience
The belief.

Lesser entries mean greater force;
You travel swift, all into my heart.
Greater force is deeper penetration;
You travel beyond, a realm unknown
So far; a nameless satiation, and a
Blissful calm, the deep sea set into the
Resplendent ripple under the warm,
Gentle Sun, free from the commotion
Of raging passion, unthreatened by
The sense of ending.
How glorious is the transfiguration of
Love, liberated from the law of
Meeting and separation!
Salvation is senses eclipsed and
Soul aglow; the enlightenment
Glows within.

My Melancholy Seeks Love

The work has wearied me, the whining
Hands refusing any action; the mind
Breaks into a yawn to inhale some
Respite, loosening its grip upon my
Being, the heart set into a sudden
Resurgence; hiatus returns to
My self—the me that craves coddling.

The two mingle into oneness that
Is aglow with a strange effulgence, the
Journey from the mundane to the sublime;
I sense within the rise of
Narcissus that rejoices in this sudden
Transfiguration, the gleam gathering in
A wide sway.

It's always a fleeting presence;
The precious is never persistent.
The heart craves, making the moment
A memory steeped in a sweet pride for
The rainy days when withered lies the
Blossom beyond nurturing and care,
And life is mere a dreamless stare.

The shutter is ready for the snapshot,
And thus is the moment frozen,
The heart beat registered

The impulse mapped, and
The utterance of silence recorded.
The symphony plays out on my face
With a magical clarity!

Such a charm is the handiwork of
Only the purest happiness, they marvel!
The radiance steals from my
Countenance in a wink;
Alas, if I had had one such who
Could tell the shade of melancholy
Behind the magic!

A Chance Visit to the Soul!

Oh, this evening why I miss
The intoxication of melancholy
In my mood, the sparkle of
Passion within, the wrench of
Pangs in the heart, the commotion of
Thoughts in the mind, and music in
My silence; Words elude my language,
Art has made a stealthy escape,
Deserting the fare of intellect;
Instead, I sense an entity blissfully calm,
Imbued with the sense of eternity.
Is it Soul?
Must be, because
Here, death feels shorn of fear.

A Seductive Imagination! (An Air Travel)

The earth of cloud, the cotton
Doughs lush and luminescent,
The same sky above,
Celestial blue, with
The ordained pristineness;
The beauty of the
Ethereal existence!

The sea of sky, crystal azure,
The water of clouds, charging forth
Upon it in a lustrous froth;
The magic of the
Celestial chimera!

At the touch of imagination
Reality mingles with fantasy;
The symphony of silence,
The serendipity of the surreal.

Dichotomy

Passion spent;
A loud lull, a blue calm,
Time frozen into a seething stillness,
And ether thinned, inane and inert.
Body, mind and heart is
A stormed affair, and senses collapse
Into a deflated float; an unbeautiful
Desert in a gloomy hurry to be the
Same sea, frenzied and foaming.
What is life if not sensations?
Nothing but a frozen lake;
Neither living nor dead!
An existence in suspension.

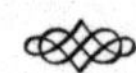

I Stay Put

Abandoned by the world,
Adopted by imagination!
The ether is rendered too thick
For the flow of the stream that
Had sprung out from the mountains
To live the promise of a cool sonorous
Sizzle and shimmery sparkle.
Fear and forlornness find
A free reign.
But destiny has a way to dodge
The human design.
Melancholy plays me to
Transmit the tremors of
Existence, and raise the throbs of
Life from a monotonous mass
In the face of the annihilation
That loomed large.
The stream is restored to its
Ordained flow with the murmurings
Of a magical mystery.

The Cloud of Tears

You look so ripe,
Why don't you rain?
The wedded earth cries out,
Parched and pained.
The cloud squirms under guilt,
Shy and shirking.
I too crave for your kiss,
The feel of your redemptive bliss,
But I am worthy of you no more,
Can't bless you with sycamore.
I am vapour of the tears
You have wept.
Inflicting on you your own tears?
Let me bear this steamy bosom,
The hapless smoke of pain.
No, rain upon me lest I should
Crack up, the earth sounds feverish;
Civilisation is the witness,
It's for the tears and tears alone
To resurrect the smiles.

The Corona Times

Death has upon man cast its stare,
Thick and fast flies the scare,
Lifeless lie such thriving roads,
That just throbbed with life in loads.

With awesome irony the air is rife,
Motions of life have ceased for life,
Distances denote concern and care,
Man submits to a tiny virus's stare.

Visits the mind Eliot's The Hollow Men,
Halting the march of my fluent pen,
For what can better explain the present
Than the mighty words of the doyen,
That this is the way the world ends
Not with a bang but a whimper.

Apocalypse looms large in the mind,
Gloom colours the soul, all unkind;
But we have survived calamities galore,
Hope returns, solid and sure;
And why will the order end humanity?
Else who is left to realise eternity?

So Corona also we shall humbly endure,
But return must to us sanity for sure;
Wise it is to celebrate eternity,

Must we not ever endeavour for divinity?
For to confuse an orange with an apple
Is to turn real the Forbidden Apple.

Lastly the Heart Speaks

Lub-dub, lub-dub,
The audible heartbeats
Haunt my silences, aborting
The coveted solitude;
A pathology that needs
Medical advice.
The doctor passes the
Electrocardiograph normal.

My miseries melt the heart kind;
It counsels—
The sighs of the dying dreams,
The cries of the unfulfilled desires,
Have loudened my beats;
I tend to beat louder in an ageing body.

The Valentine Wish

You sit in a tavern with the world
To raise the toast of wine,
Mirth sparkles, and the bearings shine,
But usher you into melancholy to
Treat with hemlock your own Valentine,
Today she is riled, resentment all red.

Swap your hemlock for wine,
I am sure the voices would be many,
Oh, it's delicious! The wine he offers us
Pales in comparison, why the whine?
Making wine tasty is utterly human,
But to render hemlock delicious
Is a magic, simply divine.
Let's swap places right away,
I wish to be this alchemist's Valentine.

My Sparkling Shore

I am wearied with the wanderings of
My heart, the constant sail shorn of
Shore; streams though I love,
Those tosses and turns, crests and
Troughs, those eerie eddies! The
Exciting sense of motion, the thrilling
Uncertainties, the spicy
Adventure that titillates the soul;
But then, good can be in excess
As well; the life-currents are conducted
Through contrasts.
The streams need to quieten into
Shores, wanderings into anchors;
Desire is never destination, but
Milestones are embedded in the journey.
But I am hankering after the shore
Where the body is serene, the
Sense sparkled, and soul titillated.
Isn't it utopia that renders reality real?

Soulbreak

The humming fan over me
As I lie on my bed
Fans some motion into
My being, stilled, and lends
Some music to my
Breaths muted;
Senses struggle to testify
To the soul that is breaking
Under the crushing burden
Of the grief from the bereavement.

It is upon the world,
Not soul, to supply life,
Life that can only furnish the force
That can get you to walk on the
Treadmill, not traverse the ground.
Life is a dream wherefrom
Man will wake up into death.

The Death Check

The road lies ahead, now
Winding no more, straight,
Undulating though, traversing
Through the flat plains; the
Ambitious hills and the mysterious
Woods are the function of youth.
My vision stops at myself atop
The last crest in sight that
Kisses the sky.
Devoid of apparition, the human
Actuality can never be absolute!

Rising from the Dead

The life-size picture of
My father, deceased not long,
Engraved on the door of my room
Suddenly meets my bleary
Eyes, as I wake up this morning.

Reason challenges the
Apparition, and I gather the
Senses in a bewildered
Hurry, the picture stays put.

The 'rising from the dead'
Flashes in an exciting stir;
Illusion and reality are the
Two faces of truth.

The Colours of My Self

Draught of physicality,
Deluge of emotions;
Enveloping void,
Inner fill;

My sensibility fertilises with your reminiscences;
Cathexis;
Agonisingly pleasant;
The thesis of love;

You are with me,
Red passions,
White ecstasy;

You are gone,
Black gloom,
Colourless tears,
Ultimately blue contentment;

White ecstasy,
Our progeny,
Potentially animate, but
Mortal ;

Blue ecstasy,
Our progeny (my sensibility fertilises with your
reminiscences),

But immortal,
Animates even the 'inanimate';

Thus the share of agony in my destiny
Is always treated with divinity,
Precluding the general due of pity,
And blessing my contentment with eternity.

Nyx and Apollo

My eyes gravitate to the horizon that
Has just begun reddening; the Sun
Proclaims its arrival with the burst of
A soft orange glow, the fascinating
Strokes on the canvas; the meditation
Is suddenly blessed with the rise of
The Sun that is scattering the
Luminous cheers across nature,
A willing prostration of a blushing
Nyx before a sanguine Apollo.

The survey of the sweep of the Sun
Guides me to the western horizon,
A sight that fills in me a disorienting
Perplexity; an orange ball, the
Mellowing fire, is set in a gliding
Descent, a spirited Nyx, the
Femme fatale, ready to engulf a
Shy Apollo.

Lamentations of a Nightingale

The rare is precious, arouses
Intense instincts for possession;
Access at the sweet will is power.
Ah, a she-nightingale that sings the
Sweetest melodies! Captured and
Encaged, its melodies to sweeten
life forever, soothe the sadness,
Perfect the pleasure.

Her sweet melodies would spring
From a hearty flight; to sing she strove
For the flight inside, her wings bruised
Every time by the bars of the cage,
Sharp and solid.

Weakened were the wings, muffled
The melodies, rancour in raptures,
Her master's ties with her ruptured;
Your notes are melodious no more,
Your globe is golden, and feed so fine?
You robbed the globe of glide—the food
Of the heart that sweetens the throat;
Unloved for ages, either I win love,
Or better my heart bleeds to redden
The rose that could win another love.

Not Missing the Rainbow

Rainbow is knowledge, common,
Rainbow is a sight, rare.
Rainbow could be wisdom;
An epiphany suddenly glows within.
Today, the rains have not blessed
The sky with a rainbow, instead the
Sky in view is a canvas exhibiting the
Random strokes of unnameable
Colours, the hues of the
Blush of clouds in the warm
Embrace of the latent Sun;
A rhythm in riots,

I am not missing the rainbow, captivated
By the charm of the beauty of
An Earthlier nature, the desire for
Symmetry in total eclipse, revelling in
The appeal of asymmetry—the
Enticement in imperfection.
I feel happiness
Closer, easier, friendlier.

The Divine Wedlock

The heart weeps when it's sad,
The heart laughs when it's happy; but
The soul sings dirge and deum at once;
I have dived into melancholy to soar,
Well-perched on the high mountains
Where the Sun warms the hostile
Snow, and the snow cools the unkind
Sun; the inevitability of pain sobers
My pleasure, the surety of pleasure
Suffuses my pain, pain and pleasure
Wedded to each other.
The mountains have blessed me with
The access to Shiva ensconced atop
The Mount Kailasha, none less than
God to solemnise this wedlock of
The opposites.
The eternal abode of such sublime
Climes I rejoice in the motherly lap of
The child of this wedlock-art, the
Embodiment of the beautied truth.

Drunk with the River

I am sitting by the river, stirred by
Its gleaming quiescence; the gentle
Winds ripple the river, a heart—the
Eternal beloved of solitude—set into the
Sweetest tones. Seeing is connecting,
And watching entering into a silent
Conversation;

I have had my share of force and frenzy
Since destiny set me down from the
Glacier, the fall from the uncertain
Mountains, and the blindness to the
Path, bestowed on me the certainty of
The energy and edge that could
Weather rocks, cut gorges and
Canyons, and amass the clay, gravel
And sand, that the knowable plains
Have shaped into the alluvial fan—
Testimony to the vigour and voyage of
Youth, the harbour of sustenance.
At forty-five, aren't you a sustainer
Like me?

The river slips into a pause, the
Winds at rest, the resplendent ripples
Settled into a lucid mirror; the sky
Inside the river, celestial azure, charms

Me into transcendence; it's the sighting
Of the communion between the earth
And the heaven.

The shift from existence to eternity
Within sets the river into a melancholic
Whisper—I know I will be fractured into
Delta, the painful creases on this
Beautiful face, before merging into
The ocean. Imagination lends wing to time;
Dyed in dusk, I rise and return
Drunk with the river.

The Tomb of a King

The tomb of the king stands stately,
The imagination and the stones
Configured into a majestic design;
Death in an enchanting radiance,
The dead come all alive in the mind.
How potent is the inanimate that
Embodies the soul of the dead, and
Immortalises the life that is no more!

The eulogy enfeebles suddenly,
The swell of the wonder nipped hard.
Immortality can as well be the
Preserve of mere lineage, devoid of
Laurels; destiny, not the deed
Has been deified!

Tryst with Divinity

The chirrups of the birds stir
The heart out of a vague inertness;
The anxieties from the reality of
Living and the conundrum of life.
Once stirred, it's more the merrier.

The heart has a way with seducing the
Senses into a pleasing submission;
The enchanting sights, the enticing
Fragrances, the soothing sounds, and
Musical silences, the titillating feel of
The cool breeze on the warming body
That is set into an effortless motion.

Tree is man's loyalest friend,
Flower the eternal beloved,
Cool breeze the instant enchantress,
Meadow the marital bed that is the
Blissful theatre for the mating of
The heart and the mind, and
The Sky emerges as the ultimate
Patriarch of the soul.
Ah how feasible is the revelatory
Moment, and accessible the tryst
With divinity!

How Can I Be Arjuna?

War is no longer
Fought with principles;
Riding on Krishna's chariot of
Wisdom, briefed on the
Primacy of evil over
Blood, and equipped with
Drona's archery skills, Arjuna
Fought against the pointed
Hands and acerbic tongues,
Right in the front.

Who will steer the
Chariot of wisdom, telling
The enemies from the gentle
Arms around my neck and
The sweet tongues by my ears?
And who will impart
The skills to fend off what
Comes from the back?

The Highway Cook

The sweat of
The dripping cook,
While he churns out
The chapatis on
The fire without,
Under the cool blaze of
Moon and neon,
Will cool the
Sparks around, and smother
The fire within.

My Earth

The celestial rulers command
High reliefs on my palms,
Squeezing a sunny sky
Right into my hands.

Navigating the universe
On my palm,
I look for my earth which
Is transfigured by the self.

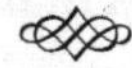

The Air is Morbid

Yet again, the scene
At this square—
The hissing haze, and
The furious fumes—
Simmers down to
The customary throngs of
The flashes and the sirens.

Floats to the fore the
Scene sighted earlier—
Men exploded into parts many,
Smeared in blood, and
Falling with a tormenting thud;
The macabre haze of
Dust and ammunition.

Strike awfully,
Flanking over the scene,
Three huge hoardings, boasting of
A friendly health insurance,
A super-specialty hospital,
And the welfare policies
Dispensing free health care.

I Wish to Be Where I Am Not

The cheerful quiver of the
Twig the bird has just left,
A soothing surge raised from
A seething stillness within;
The sonorous resonance.
I am where I am not, the
Spirit on a spirited voyage
Searching the uncertain
Destination of the bird.
I wish to dwell where I don't,
I wish to continue being
Where I am not.

Life in Flashes

The radiant red from the solitary rose
That trembles in the delicate spring
Breeze, hyacinth blushing the
Warm affection of Zephyrus, imbues
The entire green that surrounds it.

I crave for that solitary moment that
Blushes the boon by the Moirai to
Suffuse a prosaic past and
A funereal future;
My experiences promise only
An ephemeral solitary photon,
Not an enduring beam.